Furry Logic

Logic

PARENTHOOD

For Mark, Clare & Jamie.

Jane Seabrook

Furry Logic

PARENTHOOD

TEN SPEED PRESS
Berkeley | Toronto

You can't scare me. I have children.

Those who say they

sleep like babies ...

don't usually have them.

Prenatal:

When your life was still your own.

The moment

you have children,

you forgive

your parents ...

everything.

Why do they say

"*you have a baby*"?

The baby has you.

A

perfect example of

minority rule is ...

a baby in the house.

Amnesia:

A condition that enables a

woman who has been through

labor – to do it again.

Family Planning:

The art of spacing your

children the proper distance apart

to keep you on the edge of

financial disaster.

Your children look to you

for security —

so hide when you bite your nails.

Whoever said "*just say no!*"

doesn't have kids.

Why

can't you all just obey me!

Because

I'm your mother, THAT'S *why.*

Say no.

Then negotiate.

There are three ways to

get things done:

— do it yourself,

— hire someone to do it,

— or **forbid** *your kids to do it.*

When you're little,

adorable will get you

through anything.

"Ow."

The first word spoken by

children with older siblings.

Children's Property Laws:

I. *If I like it, it's mine.*

II. *If I can take it from you, it's mine.*

III. *If I had it a little while ago, it's mine.*

IV. *If it's mine, it must never appear to be yours in any way.*

V. *If it looks like mine, it's mine.*

VI. *If it's yours and I steal it, it's mine.*

VII. *If I think it's mine, it's mine.*

VIII. *If it's broken, it's yours.*

According to the child,

instant gratification takes **too long.**

Signs of Advanced Parenthood:

— *You count the sprinkles on each kid's cupcake to make sure they're equal.*

— *You hide in the bathroom just to get some alone-time.*

— *You start offering to cut up other people's food.*

The

quickest

way for

a parent

to get a

child's

attention ...

is

to

sit

down

and

look

comfortable.

If you want

your children

to listen ...

try talking softly – to someone else.

Your children are growing up when they

stop asking where they came from ...

and refuse to tell you

where they're going.

It's not

easy raising

a teenager.

Especially in the morning.

There are few things more satisfying

than seeing your children

have teenagers of their own.

You're only young once.

That is all society can stand.

Children are a great comfort

in your old age

and they help you

get there faster.

No matter

how old

a

mother is …

she continues to watch

her middle-aged children

for signs of improvement.

It's not easy getting your

grown-up kids to leave home.

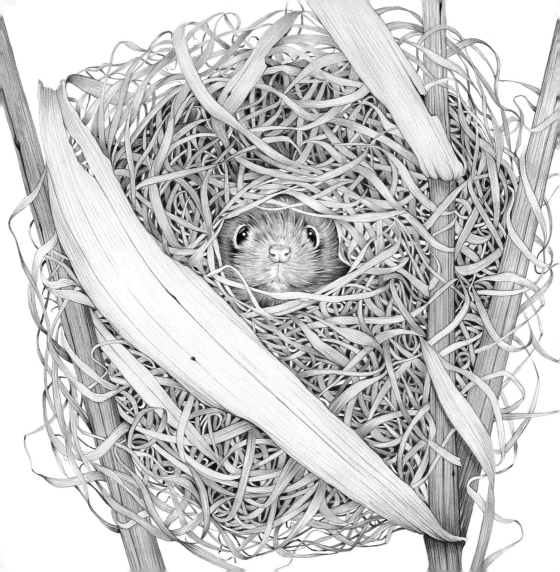

Money isn't everything.

But it sure

helps to keep

the kids in touch.

Blessed

is the parent who

expects no gratitude.

For he shall not be disappointed.

I used to have a number of theories

on raising children.

Now I have a number

of children and

no theories.

Artist's notes

No matter how many manuals on parenting we study, nothing quite prepares us for the challenges and joys of parenthood. Life is forever changed from the very moment we become parents. We find ourselves  in an unfamiliar sea of emotions, completely surrounded by an ocean of expenses!

Nevertheless, it is no coincidence that the hardest job is also the most rewarding. My kids have taught me just as much as I've ever taught them. And now that they are teenagers, I feel like I'm on the steepest learning curve of all. I have quite a few favorite lines in this book, but one that always makes me smile is this one: "Blessed is the parent who expects no gratitude. For he shall not be disappointed."

Children sometimes forget to say thank you, but if at the end of our parenting efforts they turn out to be good people, that will be thanks enough. I hope some of the pages in this book made you smile, especially if it has been one of those days when parenting didn't.

Best wishes,

Jane.

www.furrylogicbooks.com

Acknowledgments

Heartfelt thanks for all their support and encouragement to Mark Seabrook-Davison, Diana Robinson & Debby Heard. A very special thank you to Mark Seabrook-Davison who plays a vital role in helping me decide what should stay in and what should be left out of my books. I rely very much on his litmus test of what deserves to be in and more importantly, what doesn't.

Burton Silver got me started in the publishing of Furry Logic books by pointing me in the right direction, and I'm having so much fun I would like to thank him again. I would like to thank all those who have brought their expertise to this book; in particular: Troy Caltaux and Alex Trimbach at Image Centre; Debby Heard Photography; printers Ricky Cheng and Mr. Cheung at Phoenix Offset; and special thanks to Joy Willis.

Grateful thanks to John Cooney of *Grapevine* magazine for many of the quotations attributed to "Anon." Other quotations appeared or are quoted in the following publications: *Children's Property Laws: If I like it, it's mine....If it's broken it's yours.* (Anon.) in *The Penguin Dictionary of Jokes*, compiled by Fred Metcalf, Penguin Group, UK. Quotations under the following headings: *Prenatal, Amnesia, Family Planning, "Ow"* (Anon.) in *World's Best Humour*, The Five Mile Press, Melbourne, Australia. *A perfect example of minority rule is a baby in the house.* (Anon.) *Jokes, Quotes and One-Liners*, Volume Two, Thorsons, UK. *If you want your children to listen, try talking softly – to someone else.* (Anne Landers) in *Bitch!*, Michael O'Mara Books, UK.

While every effort has been made to trace copyright holders of the quotations, the publisher would be very pleased to hear from any not acknowledged here to make amends in future printings. Contact details at www.furrylogicbooks.com

Ten Speed Press
PO Box 7123, Berkeley, CA 94707
www.tenspeed.com

Distributed in Canada by Ten Speed Press Canada, in South Africa by Real Books, and in
the United Kingdom and Europe by Airlift Book Company

Library of Congress Cataloging -in-Publication Data
Seabrook, Jane.
Furry logic parenthood / Jane Seabrook.
p. cm.
ISBN 1-58008-671-3
1. Parents—Humor. 2. Parenthood—Humor. I. Title.
PN6231.P2S43 2005
818'.602—dc22   2004021296

Printed in China
First printing, 2005
1 2 3 4 5 6 7 8 9 10—09 08 07 06 05